December 2021

To
Ella, Victoria + Ivy

love
Great Aunt Leslie

✳

As we prepare for
our late May 2022
visit to the Castle,
the Banff Springs
Hotel to celebrate
great grandma
Nanny's 90th birthday.

A TIMELESS TRADITION

{ Muriel Moffat }

AFTERNOON

TEA

DOUGLAS & MCINTYRE

Douglas and McIntyre (2013) Ltd.
P.O. Box 219, Madeira Park
British Columbia, Canada, V0N 2H0
www.douglas-mcintyre.com

Cataloguing data available from Library and Archives Canada
ISBN 978-1-77100-052-9 (cloth)
ISBN 978-1-77100-053-6 (ebook)

Cover and text design by Jessica Sullivan
Printed and bound in China by C&C Offset Printing Co., Ltd.
Distributed in the U.S. by Publishers Group West

We gratefully acknowledge the financial support of the
Canada Council for the Arts, the British Columbia Arts Council,
the Province of British Columbia through the Book Publishing
Tax Credit and the Government of Canada through the
Canada Book Fund for our publishing activities.

Dedicated to
Grandma Pet, Grandma Sugar, my mother,
and to those who continue to believe
loving family traditions are the most valuable
inheritance we can leave behind.

{ CONTENTS }

ROMANCING THE TEA

. . . .

MUCH HAS BEEN written about teas and all matters relating to teas, so when I started my research, I found it curious that very little had been written about two great traditions together: the Empress Hotel and Afternoon Tea! The birth of *Afternoon Tea: A Timeless Tradition* is the result of my curiosity.

I certainly do not profess to be an expert on either subject, but I do confess my love of family and the traditions that help make them stronger and better.

Those who know me personally will be witness to the fact that I often say "must not have had an English grandmother" as the explanation or justification for a mishap, unfortunate incident or just plain lack of common sense.

My theory has always been if you didn't have an English grandmother, how could you possibly be expected to know?

Born and raised in British Columbia, always an inhabitant of Vancouver Island, the thought of not having at least one English grandmother was, to me, unimaginable. I was most fortunate in that I had an English grandmother and an English great-grandmother, on my mother's side, who lovingly nurtured, supported and instilled in me the importance of traditions and family.

Although my father's mother was also English, she is another matter entirely.

My paternal and maternal grandparents were all from England. My great-grandfather, Thomas, on my mother's side, was a British Army officer and I have many fond memories of him.

Always the English gentleman, he dressed in fine suits, white shirts, always with a tie. He had a large white handlebar moustache that was impeccably groomed. Elizabeth, his wife and my great-grandmother, very much shared his same adventurous spirit.

In 1899, Queen Victoria had recently celebrated her Diamond Jubilee when England declared war on South Africa. Great-Grandfather, with Great-Grandmother and her English china dinnerware and tea service in hand, headed to South Africa. She refused to leave England without her tea service. Those dishes traveled from England to South Africa, back to England, and then across Canada and now hold a place of honour in my china cabinet. On special occasions, I use this china and when I do, I feel their warm presence in my home. I have always joked with my family on these occasions assuring them "the grandmothers were with us."

Thomas and Elizabeth had three daughters: Mabel, Dorothy and Barbara. Mabel was my grandmother, a petite woman with snow-white hair, and sky-blue eyes set in a perfect English complexion. Although every inch a lady, and a dear one at that, she was one you did not want to cross. The fact she perpetually smelled of lavender could easily throw those who didn't know off guard.

Her teapot never got cold and she made scones so light her culinary admirers said "angels could float upon them." When asked for her secret scone recipe, she would smile sweetly and say, "Oh, it's nothing, it's just like that," and everyone knew that was all they were getting of her secret scone recipe.

She read our tea leaves with much enthusiasm on her part and great anticipation on ours and we were never disappointed.

Everyone seemed to have nicknames in those days and she, with the lavender scent, was Grandma Sugar. My great-grandmother's nickname was Grandma Pet and the two of them were my best friends growing up. I spent my summer vacations at Grandma Sugar's home and this is where I received most of my tea education.

The taking of Afternoon Tea, every day at 4:00 p.m., was something my family always did and I have wonderful memories of this from the age of four. My first tea experience was with "milk tea," which is three-quarters milk and one-quarter tea.

Grandma Pet set her tea table with the fine bone china dishes, and proper tea etiquette was shared with me from the time I could sit upright in a chair. Grandma Sugar spent hours, it seemed, teaching me how to hold a cup and saucer properly, how to handle a spoon gracefully, the proper way of eating the scones with the Devon cream and strawberry preserves and, of course, how to make pleasant conversation with one's attending company.

I am most fortunate to be able to say the belief that "children should be seen and not heard" was not part of our family ways and I have continued that philosophy with my own. The sound level at our family functions would deafen some, but I wouldn't have it any other way.

On very, very, special occasions we would go to the Empress Hotel for Sunday Afternoon Tea. The grandmas said the Empress Hotel was the place to go and the place to be seen, and it made me feel extraordinarily special. We would go to the 11:00 a.m. service at church and then on to the Empress for Afternoon Tea and, each and every time we went, it was as magical as the time before.

I would wear my best pinafore dress with white anklet socks rolled twice over to make a perfect cuff, black patent shoes, white lace gloves that took forever to put on, only to be removed the moment we stepped inside the building, as that was the proper way I had been taught and, of course, a hat, the kind with the ribbons falling from the crown, to control the hair. My hair would be rolled in rags the day before in the hopes of releasing a mass of curls for the special outing.

My grandmothers shared lots of stories about the hotel and some of the people who lived there. As a little girl, I would make believe the Empress was my very own big, beautiful castle of a home and all the people coming and going were friends and acquaintances of mine visiting from around the world because I was so important.

No matter how many times I have been to the Empress since my childhood, I continually enjoy the same feeling of "being special." I think this pleasant emotion must have been built into its stone and mortar, for I don't know of many that are not affected in the same manner.

During my lifetime, I have enjoyed tea at the Empress with four generations of my family. As a mother of four daughters and grandmother of eight, I have shared the same wonderful tradition of taking tea at the Empress with all of them. Even my grandsons have been exposed to taking tea from a very young age and, although they would probably prefer to be doing something else, they do seem to settle in and enjoy the occasion as much as we do.

To me, the tradition of taking tea is one of the greatest communication vessels ever created and certainly far more civilized than the Internet and cell phones of today's world.

This book is dedicated to all those who continue to pass down the time-honoured tradition of taking tea with the ones they love, for it is their commitment that will keep this experience alive for generations to come.

CHINA DISCOVERS TEA,
THE BRITISH MAKE IT A TRADITION

. . . .

WHAT STARTED MORE than five thousand years ago and is still popular today? If you answered "tea," you are absolutely right!

Next to water, tea is the world's most popular beverage. It is an economical libation offering endless varieties to one's palate, keeping you warm in the winter and cool in the summer. It has brought solace to millions of people, around the world, each and every day.

In 2737 BC, the Chinese Emperor Sheen Nun, who was known as the "Divine Cultivator" and the "Divine Healer," discovered tea quite by accident, so the story goes.

One afternoon, Sheen Nun was resting in his garden, sipping boiled water. His edicts required that all drinking water be boiled first, as a hygienic precaution. A few dried leaves fell from a nearby bush into his cauldron of boiling water one day, and these leaves soon emitted a delicate aroma and changed the colour of the water to brown. He was curious, decided to taste it and found himself pleasantly surprised. He instructed his servants to carefully cultivate the plant, known as *Camellia Sinensis*, a distant cousin of the camellia bush, and that was how tea was discovered.

Tea consumption spread throughout the Chinese culture, reaching into every aspect of society. From the beginning, the Chinese believed tea calmed the mind and improved thought and overall health. For many centuries, tea's purpose was solely medicinal or spiritual.

The English started drinking tea in the late 1650s when Catherine of Brogans arrived in Portsmouth, England, and asked for a cup of tea. Although not British by birth, she had married King Charles II and she had brought her tea-drinking habit from her native Portugal to England. Part of her dowry was tea packed in large chests that were transported along with her. At the time, the brewed beverage was extremely expensive, around $100 per pound, so tea was enjoyed by only the wealthy, the aristocracy and the royals.

Before tea was introduced to Britain, the English had two main meals a day: breakfast and dinner. A typical breakfast would consist of ale, bread and beef. During the 18th century, dinner was a generous meal enjoyed at the end of the day, between 7:00 p.m. and 8:30 p.m. It was found that another meal had to be introduced to provide food between the breakfast and dinner hours and, hence, lunch was founded. This lunch meal was on the light side, which left the afternoon without any refreshments, and this gap in the daily affairs of the rich and the royal is what created the tradition of Afternoon Tea.

Queen Anne introduced tea for breakfast, displacing the traditional ale. In 1840, Anna Maria, the 7th Duchess of Bedford of Woburn Abbey, Bedfordshire, England, experienced a "sinking feeling" in the late afternoon and to alleviate this discomfort, created the actual Afternoon Tea experience.

The Duchess of Bedford was known as a trendsetter in her high society circles and she, unhappy with the two meals a day, adopted the European tea service format. She would invite friends to join her for an afternoon meal, around 4:00 p.m., at her Beloit Castle estate. Small cakes, sandwiches and sweets were served with the tea.

Queen Mary's favourite time of the day was 4:00 p.m., at which time everything had to be ready for the taking of tea. Silver platters were adorned with petite sandwiches, sweets and cakes and biscuits and placed on tea trolleys: wooden crafted tables with wheels. Queen Mary herself insisted on measuring the right amount of tea leaves and adding them to the teapot to ensure the perfect pot of tea. Only after it had brewed for the required minutes, did she allow the footman to pour from the silver teapots into the fine china teacups of her guests. Her silver tea service once belonged to her favourite royal, Queen Victoria.

Afternoon Tea was very much a social event, enjoyed primarily by ladies who gathered to gossip, to discuss the latest in fashion and to be seen in the right places, at the right times and with the right company.

Alive and well once more, the traditions of Afternoon Tea have enjoyed a tremendous resurgence of popularity among all classes of society. It is an excellent way to entertain and spend time with family, friends and business associates. To take time out of our busy schedules to sit, relax and enjoy... What could possibly be better?

High tea and low tea were differentiated not only by the food that was served but by the table it was served upon. High tea was served at the dining or kitchen table and was less of a social occasion and more of a sustenance meal for the manual labourers and farmers. It was served around 7:00 or 8:00 p.m. and consisted of meats, cheeses, thick sandwiches, coddled eggs, scones, cakes and pies and was the main meal of the day.

Low tea, which eventually became Afternoon tea, was generally served from a low table, placed by the fireplace, in the parlor or sitting room and it was more of a social gathering. Its offerings were less substantial and did not include hot savories.

Whether it's high or low tea, many fond memories have been created and shared by millions who have experienced the tradition of Afternoon Tea.

3

THE ART OF MAKING
AND TAKING TEA

· · · · · · · · · · · · · · · · · · · ·

IF YOU DIDN'T have an English grandmother, you couldn't possibly be expected to know the proper way of making or taking tea, so I hope the following information is helpful to you.

TEA ETIQUETTE

⟶ Setting a proper table for tea is essential to the full tea experience. One always uses their best bone china, preferably from England. The table setting consists of cups and saucers, small side plates, cream and sugar, tongs or a spoon for sugar, lemon slices, honey and honey spoon, serving tongs for food, linen napkins and, of course, the teapot.

—◦➤ The teapot is always positioned to the right of the hostess, as she will be pouring the tea in the role of "Mother." The phrase "would you like to play Mommy" comes from this occurrence.

—◦➤ If your guest wants sugar and lemon added to their tea, the sugar should be added first. The acid of the lemon prevents the sugar from dissolving if you put it in first.

—◦➤ The cup and saucer must be picked up together, holding the saucer in one hand and the teacup in the other. Your index finger is placed through the handle of the teacup and balanced by placing the thumb on the top of the handle. Your middle finger should rest on the bottom of the handle. The teacup should be held lightly by the handle and the ring and pinkie fingers should NOT be extended in the air but, rather, should rest back towards the wrist. Arching your hand and fingers was deemed a sign of arrogance. At all times, your saucer should be held under the teacup and, without moving your head, your eyes should be lowered to the teacup and delicate sips should be taken from it.

—◦➤ If stirring of the tea is required, the spoon is not to make any noise on the inside of the teacup. Once the stirring is completed, the spoon is to be laid to the right of your teacup, on the saucer.

—•» Gloves must be removed before taking tea and, in fact, should be removed upon entering the place of tea.

—•» First and foremost, you should always temper your teapot and what that basically means is you heat your teapot first before actually brewing the tea in it. So while your water is being brought to a boil, you should fill your teapot with hot tap water and place the lid upon it. Pre-heating the teapot is much kinder to fine bone china and will ensure years of happy use without cracking.

It also will give you a better cup of tea and keep the tea hotter and longer, as the pot is already warmed.

—•» You always use fresh, cold water to make tea, never warm or hot water. Some say that distilled water makes the perfect tea. Once your water has come to a full boil, pour your hot tap water out of the teapot from the spout (to ensure the spout is also heated) and pour your boiled water into it. Add one teaspoon of good quality tea per six-ounce cup for the number of cups you wish to make and add one extra teaspoon "for the pot." Stir the tea in the pot.

—•» Allow black tea to brew for three to five minutes, green tea for three to five minutes and herbal teas for five to seven

If Teapots Could Talk

IN 1904, an enterprising Englishman, wishing to make a living doing business in Chicago, Illinois, offered over-heated business associates tea poured over ice. The United States consumes more iced tea than any other country, with 90% of tea consumption being that of iced tea.

minutes. Please keep in mind that steeping or brewing your tea for too long can extract undesirable bitterness from the leaves or teabags.

→ If using loose-leaf tea, remember that loose tea expands when it steeps, so only fill the infuser half-full. Use a strainer when pouring, if you wish, to ensure no leaves enter the teacup. If the tea is too strong, add more boiling water and if too weak, add more tea.

→ Once the tea is brewed to your taste, pour your tea into the teacups, and then add your milk and sugar to your cup. The pouring of milk into the cup before adding your tea was started in England during the 18th century; however,

Queen Elizabeth adds her milk after the tea is poured and that is how I was always taught by my English grand-mothers. Some think the same concept of tempering bone china teapots also applies to the cup; however, tea has already cooled as it was brewing and is not as hot. I sup-pose it all comes down to personal preference.

—•» A tea cozy should be placed on the teapot after the first go round of tea is poured, to ensure the following cups of tea are still hot.

WANT TO KNOW YOUR FORTUNE?

The reading of tea leaves after taking tea was very popular in England, but it was believed that fortune telling from tea leaves also originated from the Chinese. My Grandma Pet always said that gypsies were the best at it!

—•» To read one's tea leaves, you make a pot of tea, as instructed previously, and when brewed, you pour the tea into the teacups without straining the leaves. The individual drinks her cup of tea, all but the last spoonful where the leaves are. She takes the cup in her left hand and swirls it around, in a counterclockwise direction, three times.

—•» The person then turns the teacup upside down into the saucer, waits one minute and removes the cup, leaving the tea leaves on the saucer.

—⟶ A skillful tea leaf reader will be able to read the symbols and images made by the tea leaves and foresee the owner's future. The handle of the teacup represents the person and the readings always begin at the left of the handle and proceed around the cup in the same direction.

—⟶ Leaves farthest from the handle are events in the physical distance, leaves closest to the rim are the present and the tea leaves closest to bottom of the cup represent the future.

What you want to see in your tea leaves are depictions of certain shapes, such as a cow, bird, star, tree or dog, as they all mean good fortune.

4

AFTERNOON TEA AT
THE FAIRMONT EMPRESS

. . . .

ℱROM THE MOMENT the doors opened on January 20th, 1908, the Empress Hotel, known now as the Fairmont Empress, has been skillfully upholding the tradition of Afternoon Tea and, in doing so, she became the favourite venue for various members of my family during the past century.

Although most visitors think Fairmont bought the Canadian Pacific Hotels, it is in fact the other way around. In 1999, Canadian Pacific Hotels purchased 64% of the Fairmont and Delta Hotels and Resorts properties. It was determined for marketing purposes the name "Fairmont" was known more globally than Canadian Pacific, sadly

If Teapots Could Talk

JOHN ROWLAND, the "official lobby sitter" and a lovely older gentleman, was a music lover. He sat in the lobby for about thirty years listening to the Billy Trickle Trio and talking to guests and locals. It is said he never spent a dime in the hotel.

true, so the Empress became the Fairmont Empress. Aside from the name change, everything else seems to have stayed, thankfully, the same.

Both Grandma Pet and Grandma Sugar enjoyed tea in the beautiful Palm Court of the Empress and proudly boasted being two of the few who ever did. The Palm Court is the room adjacent to the Tea Lobby that boasts a spectacular domed, stained-glass ceiling. They said the Palm Court was originally designed to be the Tea Room but it was found to be "acoustically unacceptable." The elliptical ceiling had created a whispering gallery, which meant that sound produced at certain points in the room could be heard quite clearly in other distant points in the room, and so guests had to whisper for fear of being overheard. The Afternoon Tea service was quickly relocated to the hotel's lobby, for after all, what was the point of taking tea if one couldn't talk?

Like the kitchen is to a home, the lobby is the heart of a hotel, and it was the perfect place for people to gather, to be seen and to watch others. Careers were lost and launched, reputations built and crushed, relationships broken and formed, family matters discussed and resolved or made worse... all during the Afternoon Teas in the lobby of the Empress Hotel.

The Royal Restoration of 1989 gave the Empress a new wing, which included a new, modern lobby, and the original lobby was renamed the Tea Lobby. Afternoon Tea continued to be served there, only without the hustle and bustle of guests coming and going, which made it an even more serene experience.

The mere size of the Tea Lobby is enough to make you realize you are somewhere removed from the ordinary. The Victorian era, in its opulence and priority, can surely be felt in your veins when in this great room. I know I sit and walk taller when I am there. A portrait of Queen Mary and a portrait of King George v, placed at either end of the room above the two grand fireplaces as though facing one another, give the feeling you just joined them for tea! Oversized windows across the entire outside wall of the room provide everyone with a picture-postcard view of Victoria's magnificent Inner Harbour.

The room exudes significance and comfort: loveseats, high-back leather and upholstered chairs, rich mahogany tables of various shapes and heights, lots of room between tables that are positioned in a scattered rather than institutional way so as always to provide privacy to each table, tapestry carpets over original wooden floors and exquisite flower arrangements. There are large, wide, beveled-glass French doors leading out to a wonderful private verandah across the front of the Tea Lobby that is open only during the high season. It is one of my favourite places to be in the hotel and if you get an opportunity to try it, you definitely should.

Unless you have an unusual request, the process of tea is entirely taken care of by your highly competent tea server, some of whom have been practicing the art of serving tea for over twenty-five years. Looking at menus, having to make decisions, only takes away from the complete repose of sitting back and being waited on.

The tea is prepared to your preference and a three-tiered cake stand full of wonderful foods is introduced to you by your server. Although the individual items change periodically, the theme seems to remain constant.

Tea begins with seasonal fresh fruit to cleanse your palate, topped with Chantilly cream, of course; finger sandwiches of five varieties; scones the Empress is famous for, decadently enjoyed with Devon clotted cream and strawberry preserves imported from England; and, if that is not enough, sweets, such as lemon curd tarts, chocolate eclairs and truffles, crème puffs and more, top the cake stand. Never feel embarrassed asking for a takeaway container for the food you cannot consume. Many people think it inappropriate to ask because they are at the Empress but not so! They have containers specifically for this purpose.

You are never hurried through tea and your server seems to magically appear only when more tea is required to be poured; otherwise, you are left alone to enjoy your company, take care of business or simply relax and appreciate the surroundings and the opportunity to go back in time to when we had time and took the time!

Musical interludes have always been enjoyed during tea and today it is the sounds of the various pianists at the grand piano that provide the perfect background music. During the Christmas season, songs by carolers dressed in Victorian costumes delight both the eyes and the ears and there are also special performances by several of the local school choirs. Put all that together with the magic of the

If Teapots Could Talk

WEALTHY LADIES of leisure, many of them widowed, known as the "Empress Dowagers," lived permanently at the hotel. The cost then: $310 per month with meals, $60 without meals. Florence French lived at the Empress for forty-two years.

During the depression of the '30s, many of these ladies moved up to the sixth and seventh floors, built originally as the maid's quarters, for the cost of $1 a day. They did their best to economize but somehow they managed to emerge to the lobby for the famous Afternoon Tea. One elderly lady was known for her habit of only ordering a pot of hot water and ever-so-discreetly adding her own teabag to the pot when no one was looking, so as not to be charged and yet to still be able to enjoy the experience.

Festival of Trees that is also ever-present throughout the hotel during that time, and it makes it one of my family's favourite annual outings.

AN EXCLUSIVE BLEND OF TEA

Although there is no question the food enjoyed during tea is important, the tea itself is the essence of the experience. The Empress has its own special blend, the Empress blend, four black and one green, created exclusively for them by an expert tea merchant.

By blending teas from different regions of the world, the Empress's tea merchant boasts the ability to provide a tea product that remains consistent from one pot to the next and that is not only impressive but of the utmost importance.

Acknowledging that superb tea quality was usually related to loose-leaf tea, the Empress tea merchant discovered if they slowed down the speed of the teabagging machinery, the large loose-leaf tea could be packaged in bags without impacting the quality of the blend.

The Empress Tea Lobby uses teabags, not loose leaf, for their tea service, and I have never enjoyed a better cup of tea anywhere else.

VERY SPECIAL CHINA!

The Empress understands, like Grandma Pet, the importance of using only your very best china for the tea service. The china pattern used since 1998 for Afternoon Tea and on the Gold Floor of the hotel is called the Royal China and it is rich with history. The original pattern was presented to King George V in 1914 to commemorate the opening of the Booth Factory in Stoke, England. This regal pattern was first used at the Empress in 1939 for the Royal visit of King George VI and Queen Elizabeth (the Queen Mother).

Silver teapots keep the tea piping hot and, once adorned with the blue tea mitt proudly displaying the Empress heraldic badge, the tea mitt itself makes an interesting conversation piece because few have any idea what the blue triangular object is for. As I had my English grand-mothers to educate me, I knew the first time I saw it. The server places the loop of the tea mitt around the knob on the teapot lid, twists it into place, and then the body of the mitt goes down over the handle itself. It stops the serv-er's hand from getting burnt. Very logical when you think about it!

The Empress badge itself is certainly worthy of men-tion for it drew much local and global media attention, not to mention the sound of tongues clicking when it was dis-covered the Empress had been doing something improper!

For years the hotel used a copy of the Imperial State Crown as her official hotel emblem, and this was eventu-ally discovered and denounced as quite a "no-no." The only one entitled to use the crown of sovereignty is the sover-eign itself, and the Empress was not part of sovereignty.

All crowns other than those of sovereignty must be coronets, which, unlike crowns, are not closed in at the top.

Having received the appropriate reprimands by the Crown, a heraldic badge, created by the Chief Herald of Canada, Robert Watt, in accordance with accepted symbols of western heraldry, many dating back to the Middle Ages, was granted by the Crown to the hotel on September 28th, 1999, and has been proudly used as the hotel's emblem ever since.

My mother once commented that she found it ironic that something that got them into hot water, so to speak, was later displayed on an object called a tea mitt, which was designed to keep one away from the hot water!

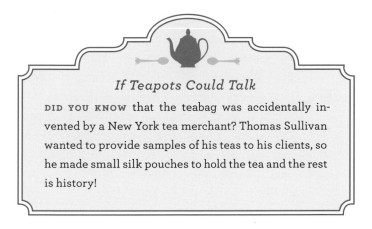

If Teapots Could Talk

DID YOU KNOW that the teabag was accidentally invented by a New York tea merchant? Thomas Sullivan wanted to provide samples of his teas to his clients, so he made small silk pouches to hold the tea and the rest is history!

These ladies are wearing hobble dresses which were very popular to wear to tea during 1910–1911. The fashion of the time required the bottom of the hobble dress to be tightly closed, which made walking gracefully very difficult. However, fashion was more important than comfort, so ladies would practice in private, placing a corded rope between their knees under their hobble dress and taking small steps until they got it right. The colours of the time were soft. Gloves and hats were mandatory for ladies of all ages and for some years the fashion in hats was the bigger the better! Mandy Kray, owner of WalkAbout Tours, confesses they had their hobble dresses made with the bottom's open, not closed.

Tea gowns enjoyed tremendous popularity from 1875 through to the 1920s and were worn by the hostess when entertaining guests at home for tea. This was the time when most husbands were out and about taking care of business while their wives entertained without them. The tea gowns were made of filmy chiffon or fine silk, trimmed with an abundance of lace and often free of corsetry, which afforded women great comfort and a tremendous sense of femininity, all the while fueling the gossip of what was going on behind tea doors at these private gatherings. None of my family members have ever confessed to owning a tea gown!

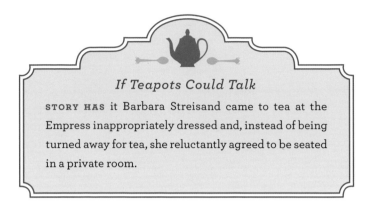

If Teapots Could Talk

STORY HAS it Barbara Streisand came to tea at the Empress inappropriately dressed and, instead of being turned away for tea, she reluctantly agreed to be seated in a private room.

Much to the disappointment of many, the dress code for Afternoon Tea at the Empress has been greatly relaxed in order to accommodate today's guests. Described now as "smart casual," this means no torn jeans, short shorts, beachwear or flip-flops; jogging pants or tank tops and everything else is okay!

Personally, I feel getting dressed up for the occasion adds to the whole tea experience. My family and I enjoy "putting on the Ritz," as Grandma Sugar used to say! After all, how many times are you going to attend Afternoon Tea at the Empress?

RECIPES

· · · · · · · · · · · · ·

EGG SALAD SANDWICH

1 tbsp. mayonnaise

½ green onion (diced)

2 hard-boiled eggs (peeled and chopped)

salt & pepper to taste

2 tsp. butter

2 slices multigrain bread

1 Add 1 tbsp. mayonnaise and ½ green onion to chopped hard-boiled eggs.

2 Add seasoning.

3 Butter two slices of multigrain bread.

4 Put egg mixture onto one slice and top with other slice.

5 Cut off crusts and cut sandwich into preferred sizes.

If an egg falls and smashes, it foretells
of good news but if it is only damaged or cracked,
then bad luck will find you instead.

{ SMOKED SALMON SANDWICH }

1 tsp. cream cheese

1 tsp. mayonnaise

1 tsp. fresh dill

salt & pepper to taste

2 slices rye bread

4 slices smoked salmon

1 Blend together cream cheese and mayonnaise, add fresh dill and season to taste.
2 Spread mixture onto each slice of rye bread.
3 Add smoked salmon and roll up.
4 Slice and serve.

*If the cook cuts bread in an
uneven fashion, it is said to be a sure
sign that lies have been told.*

CARROT AND GINGER SANDWICH

1 carrot (grated)

1 tbsp. cream cheese (softened)

1 tbsp. mayonnaise

½ tsp. ginger paste (sweet)

salt & pepper to taste

2 tsp. butter

2 slices light rye bread

1 Blend together grated carrot, cream cheese, mayonnaise and ginger paste.
2 Add salt and pepper to taste.
3 Butter both pieces of light rye bread.
4 Place carrot mixture onto one slice and top with other slice of bread.
5 Cut off crusts and cut sandwich into preferred sizes.

{ CURRIED CHICKEN SANDWICH }

200 grams (7½ oz.) boneless, skinless chicken leg

½ medium onion, sliced

1 tsp. curry powder

¼ tsp. sage, chopped

¼ tsp. basil, chopped

oil to coat chicken

2 tsp. mango chunks

salt & pepper to taste

2 tsp. butter

3 slices rye bread

1 Preheat oven to 425°F.

2 Put chicken, onion, curry powder and herbs in a bowl.

3 Mix well with enough oil to lightly coat the chicken.

4 Spread onto baking tray and roast for 20 minutes a pound.

5 Allow to cool.

6 Put chicken mixture into food processor and chop to a chunky consistency (if there is juice in roasting pan, add it to the mixture).

7 Add mango and season to taste.

8 Butter both slices of bread.

9 Spread mixture on one piece of rye, top with second piece of bread, spread another layer of chicken and top with third piece of rye.

10 Cut off crusts and cut sandwich into preferred sizes.

{ SHRIMP MOUSSE ON BAGUETTE }

200 grams (7½ oz.) baby shrimp

½ tsp. chives, chopped

1 tbsp. mayonnaise

1 tsp. ketchup

splash of brandy (to your taste)

¼ tsp. celery salt

salt & pepper to taste

sliced baguette of your choice

1 Squeeze shrimp well to remove liquid.

2 Take half the shrimp and purée to a smooth paste in a food processor.

3 Take other half of shrimp and chop coarsely.

4 Add remaining ingredients and mix well.

5 Season to taste.

6 Use large piping tip to pipe mousse onto baguette.

7 Garnish with finely diced fruit or herbs.

CUCUMBER SANDWICH

2 tsp. butter

2 tsp. mayonnaise

*pinch of horseradish (optional)

2 slices white bread

3 English cucumbers (peeled and thinly sliced)

salt & pepper to taste

1 Spread the butter and mayonnaise on both slices of bread.
2 Add thinly sliced cucumber to one slice of bread.
3 Add seasoning to cucumbers.
4 Top with the other slice of bread.
5 Cut off crusts and cut sandwich into preferred sizes

* In recent years, the Empress has added some horse-radish to the mayonnaise to give the sandwich a bit of a bite, but this is purely optional. The very traditional British cucumber sandwich did not have this.

{ FRUIT TARTLETS }

PASTRY DOUGH	PASTRY CREAM
1¾ cups flour	6 yolks
7 tbsp. butter, diced	2 tbsp. granulated sugar
1 cup icing sugar, sifted	4½ tbsp. flour
Pinch of salt	2 cups milk
2 eggs at room temperature	1 vanilla bean, split
	1 tbsp. butter

PASTRY DOUGH

1 Preheat oven to 375°F.

2 Sift flour onto work surface and form a well in the center.

3 Put in butter and work it with your fingertips until very soft.

4 Add the sugar and salt, mix well, then add the eggs and mix again.

5 Gradually draw the flour into the mixture to make a homogeneous paste.

6 Knead the paste, roll into a ball and refrigerate for several hours before using.

7 With a rolling pin, on a floured surface, roll out the dough to about ⅛″ thickness.

8 Cut your desired shape to fit the aluminum tart cups and fill small paper cups with beans and insert them into the moulds.

9 Bake for 10–15 minutes or until golden in colour.

PASTRY CREAM

1 In a bowl, mix the yolks and half the sugar.

2 Sift the flour and mix into the above.

3 In a saucepan, bring the milk, other half of sugar and vanilla bean to a boil, stirring continuously.

4 Take a cup of the hot milk and stir into the bowl with the flour mixture and then return this to cook in the saucepan to thicken.

5 Add the butter.

6 Pour into a container and cover with plastic wrap directly on top to prevent skin from forming.

7 When cool, fill tart shells with pastry cream, then top with fruit and cover lightly with apricot glaze.

Makes 2 dozen or 3 dozen, depending on the size of your tart shells

{ EMPRESS SCONES }

2 lbs. 4 oz. (8½ cups) flour

9 oz. (1 cup + 2 tsp.) butter (hard)

9 oz. (1 cup + 2 tsp.) sugar

2 oz. (4 tbsp.) baking powder

pinch of salt

5½ eggs*

6 oz. (¾ cup) raisins

16 oz. (2 cups) whipping cream

1 Preheat oven to 350°F.

2 Crumb flour, butter, sugar, baking powder and salt.

3 Add eggs* slowly.

4 Add raisins.

5 Add cream and mix to create a smooth dough.

6 Roll out to ½" thickness and cut into desired size and shape.

7 Brush scones with egg yolk and bake for 25–30 minutes.

* The recipe actually uses 6 eggs. Separate the 6th egg
   and add the white half of the 6th egg into the batter;
   the yellow half of the 6th egg is used to do the egg wash.

Makes 35 scones

SCOTTISH SHORTBREAD

325 grams (1½ cups) granulated sugar

750 grams (3⅓ cups) unsalted butter

225 grams (2⅜ cups) pastry flour

750 grams (7⅞ cups) bread flour

12 grams (1 tbsp.) salt

9 grams (2 tsp.) vanilla extract

1 Cream butter and sugar together.

2 Sift both flours, add salt and vanilla and combine.

3 Spread mixture evenly onto a sheet pan and refrigerate.

4 Cut dough into desired shape.

5 Bake at 400°F for 15–20 minutes.

Makes 2 dozen

*Bad luck will always follow the spilling
of salt, unless a pinch of salt is thrown over the
left shoulder, directly into the face of the Devil,
who caused the trouble in the first place!*

A͡N ENGLISH CRUMPET is a cake made from flour or potato and yeast, eaten mainly in England, and dates back to 1694. It is circular in shape and has a flat top covered in small holes. It is spongy in texture and bland in taste and that is why crumpets are best when served hot and covered in butter, with honey, jam, marmalade or maple syrup!

The first recipe for crumpets was cooked
like a pancake and contained no eggs.
They were the mainstay of food
for the middle-class workers of England!

{ THE FAMOUS ENGLISH CRUMPET }

½ oz. dry yeast

1 tsp. sugar

3½ cups warm water

4 cups flour

2 tbsp. baking powder

1½ tsp. salt

1 Heat griddle to 450°F.

2 Dissolve yeast and sugar in warm water.

3 Mix together flour, baking powder and salt.

4 Add to yeast and whisk together until well blended.

5 Grease inside of crumpet rings.

6 Place rings on heated griddle and pour in ¾ cup of batter.

7 Cook until bubbles form and the top is dry.

8 Remove rings and turn the crumpet over to brown.

Makes 2 dozen, and leftovers can be toasted!

{ MAIDS OF HONOUR }

PASTRY	FILLING	ICING
1 cup pastry flour	½ cup sugar	½ cup icing sugar
¼ tsp. salt	1 stick of butter	1 tsp. almond essence
1 cup butter	2 eggs (½ cup)	2 tsp. water
Cold water to mix (allow 8–12 tsp.)	2 tsp. almond essence	glacé cherries
	2 tbsp. ground almonds	
	raspberry jam	

PASTRY

1 Preheat oven to 325°F.
2 Mix flour and salt together and cut in butter until mixture resembles fine crumbs.
3 Add water, a little at a time, and mix well until dough is formed.
4 Roll out dough onto floured surface to 1″ thickness and cut into rounds and put into tart tins.

FILLING

1 Cream sugar and butter until cream coloured.
2 Add eggs and beat well.

3 Add 2 tsp. almond essence, then ground almonds and beat well.

4 Place small amount of jam into each pastry shell and fill with almond mixture.

5 Bake for 20 minutes.

ICING

1 Mix icing sugar with 1 tsp. almond essence and a little water to make a glaze to spread on tarts once they have cooled. Garnish with glacé cherry.

Makes 2 dozen

The name of this sweet is said
to have come from the maids of honour
who attended Elizabeth I
when she lived in Richmond Palace!

{ BANBURY TARTS }

FILLING	PASTRY
1 cup seedless raisins, chopped	3 cups pastry flour
1 cup sugar	1 tsp. salt
1 egg slightly beaten	1 cup shortening
1 tbsp. saltine crackers, rolled	4 tbsp. ice water
juice and rind of 1 lemon	1-2 tbsp. milk

1 Preheat oven to 400°F.

2 Mix all of the filling ingredients together and set aside to prepare pastry.

3 Mix flour and salt and cut in shortening with a pastry blender or two knives until mixture comes together in pea-sized nuggets.

4 Add water, 1 tbsp. at a time, using only what is needed to hold the dough together.

5 Roll onto floured board as for piecrust and cut into 3½″ rounds.

6 Moisten around the edges with milk.

7 Place a tablespoon of the filling on one side of the rounds and fold over.

8 Press the edges together and prick the tops.

9 Bake on a greased cookie sheet for 15-20 minutes.

Makes 1 dozen

{ QUEEN MARY'S LEMON CURD }

10 egg yolks

4¼ cups white sugar

1½ cups + 2 tbsp. fresh lemon juice

½ tsp. salt

½ lb. butter

peel of 4 lemons

1 packet of gelatin

1 tbsp. cold water

1 Combine egg yolks, sugar and lemon juice in heavy-bottomed saucepan.
2 Stir mixture over medium heat until almost to a boil.
3 Add remaining ingredients and stir well.
4 Blend gelatin in cold water and dissolve over low heat.
5 Add to hot mixture.
6 Stir and strain.

Makes 40 servings
Lemon curd is a very English tradition, which can be served warm or cold on scones or toast or used as a filling for tarts or cakes.

{ CLOTTED CREAM }

2 gallons of milk from
a Jersey or Guernsey cow
(the milk from these cows
has a higher butterfat content
and makes the best cream)

1 Let the milk stand overnight in a large metal pan.
2 Next morning, slowly heat or scald the milk for one hour. Do not boil milk. During this time, a semi-firm, thick, yellow crust of cream will form on the surface.
3 After the hour is up, remove pan from heat and place in a cold room, taking care not to disturb the crust that has formed on the milk.
4 Leave to cool for 12 hours and then skim off the clotted cream crust with a wide knife.

Serve cold in a crystal bowl. The proper way to use is to spread the cream on a homemade scone, followed by a lashing of strawberry jam.

{ MOCK DEVONSHIRE CREAM }

(when you can't get the real thing!)

4 oz. cream cheese (softened)

1 tbsp. white sugar

1 cup whipping cream

1 Blend cream cheese and sugar together.
2 Stir in whipping cream and beat with mixer until stiff.
3 Store covered in fridge for up to one week.

In Irish folklores and superstitions, there is something called "nipping the cake." The custom was to break off a small piece of cake when fresh from the oven to avert bad luck and ward off the wee people, who were known to be mischievous!

．．．．．．．．．．．．．．．．．．

）（ WAS INTRODUCED to these "cookies" when I went to visit my good friend in San Francisco. It was during American Thanksgiving and Avril told me she had made me some cookies.

I'm not sure what Russia or cakes have to do with these unbelievable melt-in-your-mouth better-than-shortbreads, but they will surely become one of your favourites for holidays and special occasions.

When describing them, my friend Julia says they are like the restaurant scene from *When Harry Met Sally!* I dare you to eat only one!

RUSSIAN TEA CAKES

1 cup soft butter

½ cup sifted confectioner's (icing) sugar

1 tsp. vanilla extract

2¼ cups cake flour

½ tsp. salt

¾ cup chopped pecans

confectioner's sugar for coating

1 Preheat oven to 350°F.

2 Cream butter, sugar and vanilla together.

3 Mix flour and salt, then blend into creamed butter mixture.

4 Stir in nuts.

5 Cover and chill in refrigerator for 20 minutes.

6 Once chilled, roll into balls, about 1–1½" thick, and place on greased cookie sheet.

7 Bake for 15–20 minutes and watch carefully that they do not burn. They will not appear cooked when they come out, but they harden as they cool, so don't overbake. When the bottoms are golden brown they are ready!

8 Let them cool and then roll in more confectioner's sugar coating so they are white.

Makes about 2 dozen and surprisingly freeze beautifully. You can eat them right from the freezer!

· · · · · · · · · · · · · · · · · · · ·

T̲RIFLE HAS A history dating back to the mid 1700s and the name was derived from a Middle English word, "trufle," that initially originated from the French word "trufe," which means something of little importance.

The first trifle was made from stale sponge cake soaked in wine in a large bowl topped with leftover custard and fruit. Remember, there was no refrigeration in those days, so the trifle was created to use up all the stale cakes, cookies and biscuits!

{ THE FAMOUS ENGLISH TRIFLE }

CAKE

5 eggs

2/3 cup sugar

1 cup flour

SYRUP

3 tbsp. water

3 tbsp. sugar

3 tbsp. sherry

1 tbsp. rum

CUSTARD

2 egg yolks

1 egg

¼ cup sugar

1 tbsp. cornstarch

1½ cups milk

TRIFLE LAYER

1 cup black-
currant jam

WHIPPED CREAM

1 cup whipping cream

1 tbsp. white sugar

1 tbsp. icing sugar

1 tsp. vanilla extract

FRUIT & NUTS

1 cup raspberries

¼ cup sliced
almonds

¼ cup chopped
pistachio nuts

CAKE

1 Preheat oven to 350°F.

2 Lightly grease and flour a 9 × 9 × 2″ baking pan for
   sponge cake.

3 In large mixing bowl, beat the 5 eggs at high speed
   for 4 minutes or until thick.

4 Gradually add the ²/₃ cup of sugar and beat for
   4-5 minutes more or until light and fluffy.

5 Fold in the flour.

6 Pour batter into greased pan and bake for 20 minutes.

7 Remove and let cool.

continued overleaf. . .

SYRUP

1 Place water and sugar in saucepan and bring to a boil.
2 Remove from heat and add sherry and rum.
3 Cool to room temperature.

CUSTARD

1 Beat together the yolks and one egg and set aside.
2 In saucepan, add ¼ cup sugar and cornstarch and stir in milk.
3 Cook over medium heat until it thickens and then remove from heat.
4 Gradually add the beaten egg mixture and stir and cook until bubbly, but do not boil.
5 Reduce heat and cook for 2 more minutes.
6 Remove from heat and let cool.

BUILDING THE TRIFLE

1 Split cake in half horizontally and spread bottom layer of cake with jam.
2 Replace the top cake layer on top.
3 Cut cake into ¾″ cubes and place in large glass bowl.
4 Pour the syrup over the cake.
5 Pour custard over cake.
6 Cover and let chill overnight.

WHIPPED CREAM

1 Beat together whipping cream, white sugar, icing sugar and vanilla until stiff peaks form.
2 Smooth whipping cream over top of trifle.
3 Garnish with almonds, nuts and raspberries.

Makes 10–12 servings

{ ECCLES CAKES }

1¾ cups flour

2¼ tsp. baking powder

1 tbsp. sugar

¼ tsp. salt

¼ cup butter

2 eggs, beaten

⅓ cup half-and-half cream

2 tbsp. currants

1 tsp. butter

2 tbsp. sugar

cinnamon to taste

1 Preheat oven to 450°F.
2 Mix together flour, baking powder, sugar and salt.
3 Cut in butter until mixture resembles coarse oatmeal.
4 Beat eggs and set aside 2 tsp. of the beaten egg and mix remaining egg with cream.
5 Make a well in the center of the flour mixture and add egg and cream mixture and mix just enough to form dough.
6 Turn dough out to ¾″ thickness.

7 Using a biscuit cutter, cut 2½" rounds and place on a greased baking sheet 2 inches apart.

8 Poke a hole in the center of each round and fill with 1 tsp. currants and a dollop of butter.

9 Pinch edges of circle together in center of cake and brush tops with reserved egg.

10 Mix sugar and cinnamon together and sprinkle on top.

11 Bake for 10–12 minutes or until golden in colour.

Makes 6 cakes and should be served warm

．．．．．．．．．．．．．．．．．．．

S ALLY LUNN WAS a young French refugee who arrived in Bath, England, more than three hundred years ago, and she created a special taste in a light bun that could be enjoyed either as a sweet or savory. The cakes were rich, round and large, and her admirers often referred to them as "Sally's Buns." The franchise Sally Bun was started with her in mind.

Many cooks believe that food mixed in anything but a clockwise direction will never taste good! The saying "East to west is always best" is proof of this and said to have originated from ancient peoples who worshipped the sun and believed that all important functions of life must be conducted in an east-to-west direction.

SALLY LUNN CAKE

1 cup hot milk

¼ lb. butter

⅓ cup sugar

1 tsp. salt

1 tbsp. dry yeast

3½ cups warm water

3 eggs

3½ cups white flour

1 Preheat oven to 425°F.

2 Mix hot milk, butter, sugar, and salt in large bowl and let mixture cool to lukewarm.

3 Stir yeast into warm water and let stand for 5 minutes until dissolved.

4 Add yeast and eggs to first mixture and beat vigorously, gradually adding in flour.

5 Cover and let rise until double in size.

6 Place dough in a tube pan and bake for 50 minutes.

ACKNOWLEDGEMENTS

. . . .

OUR HEARTFELT THANKS to the Fairmont Empress Hotel for sharing so generously some of the recipes past and present from Afternoon Tea. Other recipes included are passed-down treasures from family and friends.

If not for the generosity and support of the hotel, most particularly the staff of the Tea Lobby and the Fairmont Store and Mandy Kray, owner of WalkAbout Tours, this book would not have been possible. To this end, I want to say thank you, most sincerely, and offer the following information on their behalf.

AFTERNOON TEA AT THE FAIRMONT EMPRESS

For Afternoon Tea, daily, 365 days of the year, with few exceptions (the room is occasionally booked out for movie filming and private events), seatings start from 12:00 p.m. The number of seatings, times and costs all vary according to season.

Reservations are required: locally (250) 389-2727; within North America 1-800-257-7544; internationally (506) 863-6310 or www.fairmont.com.

THE FAIRMONT STORE

Located directly across from the Tea Lobby, the store carries lots of delightful items, including the Royal China and the world famous Empress teas. Phone (250) 385-7730; fax (250) 385-7733; email emp.fairmontstore@fairmont.com. Hours of operation vary according to season.

Most, although not all, Fairmont hotels offer Afternoon Tea and a Fairmont Store—the Fairmont website, www.fairmont.com, would tell you more.

WALKABOUTS HISTORICAL TOURS

Informative and entertaining, WalkAbouts Historical Tours offers daily tours of the world famous Fairmont Empress Hotel.

Phone (250) 592-9255; email walkabouts@shaw.ca; www.walkabouts.ca.